BUSES OF BERKSHIRE AND HAMPSHIRE
PAST AND PRESENT

Richard Stubbings

AMBERLEY

Bibliography

Booth, Gavin, *Bus Operators 1970: The South East and Eastern Counties of England* (Hersham: Ian Allan Publishing Ltd, 2005)
Booth, Gavin, *Britain's Last Municipal Operators* (Hersham: Ian Allan Publishing Ltd, 2012)
Lyons, Mark, *The Go-Ahead Group* (Hersham: Ian Allan Publishing Ltd, 2012)
Witton, A. M. and Telfer, R. L., *Fleetbook 11 Buses of South-East England* (Manchester: A. M. Witton, 1977 and 1980)

First published 2026

Amberley Publishing
The Hill, Stroud
Gloucestershire, GL5 4EP

www.amberley-books.com

Copyright © Richard Stubbings, 2026

The right of Richard Stubbings to be identified as the Author of this work has been asserted in accordance with the Copyrights, Designs and Patents Act 1988.

ISBN 978 1 3981 1754 9 (print)
ISBN 978 1 3981 1755 6 (ebook)

All rights reserved. No part of this book may be reprinted or reproduced or utilised in any form or by any electronic, mechanical or other means, now known or hereafter invented, including photocopying and recording, or in any information storage or retrieval system, without the permission in writing from the Publishers.

British Library Cataloguing in Publication Data.
A catalogue record for this book is available from the British Library.

Origination by Amberley Publishing.
Printed in the UK.

Appointed GPSR EU Representative: Easy Access System Europe Oü, 16879218
Address: Mustamäe tee 50, 10621, Tallinn, Estonia
Contact Details: gpsr.requests@easproject.com, +358 40 500 3575

Contents

Introduction	4
Reading	5
Bracknell	23
Farnborough and Aldershot	33
Winchester	48
Southampton	60
Gosport	72
Portsmouth and Southsea	77

Introduction

In 1974 there was a big change in my life with a move away from my beloved Somerset to the South East when my father took a new post near Guildford. What I found in Surrey's county town and the surrounding area will be covered in a later volume. Suffice to say, however, that the move away from the West Country did bring a wide variety of new bus-spotting opportunities, particularly as I was by then gradually beginning to do more bus photography. Berkshire and Hampshire, counties adjacent to my new home in Surrey, brought a mix of former Tilling operations in the form of Hants & Dorset and former BET operators such as Southdown in the Portsmouth area. Linking these two was Alder Valley, combining the former Tilling company Thames Valley with the former BET company Aldershot & District. Then there were the three large municipal companies in Reading, Southampton and Portsmouth, as well as the operations of Provincial around Gosport and Fareham. Independent operators were in the main in the Reading area with firms like Chiltern Queens and around Winchester with the famous King Alfred company, which, by the time of my arrival in the South East, had become part of Hants & Dorset. It could therefore be said that there were some compensations for leaving Somerset!

I have tried to illustrate the variety of vehicles that I recall from my visits to these places reaching back to the mid-1970s. There are, inevitably, omissions as one can only really scratch the surface and give a flavour of the times. Where I have used photographs of preserved vehicles this is because, whilst I recall seeing them in service, I never got to photograph them. Where photographic quality is less than ideal it is because of the standard of the camera used (my first camera was a cheap instamatic) and youthful inexperience. For this I apologise. I must acknowledge the assistance of Wikipedia for helping to fill in large gaps in my knowledge, particularly regarding ownership of companies after deregulation. I must also thank my long-suffering partner Debs for helping me with some research, reading through my ramblings here, accompanying me on photographic expeditions and allowing the use of some of her photographs.

Reading

Berkshire and its county town of Reading are, by nature of their proximity to London with frequent rail services into Paddington and Waterloo, popular with commuters who wish to avoid living in London. Reading is a historic town with a ruined twelfth-century abbey, once one of the richest royal monasteries in Europe. It was founded by King Henry I, who is also buried there. Reading is also the home of the prison where the poet Oscar Wilde was incarcerated and where he wrote his 'Ballad of Reading Gaol'. Reading is also, at the time of writing, the home of one of the few remaining municipally owned bus companies in the country, Reading Transport Ltd, trading as Reading Buses. The origins of the company go back to the late 1870s when Reading Tramways was formed, being taken over by the municipal authorities in 1901. The last trams ran before the Second World War, being replaced by both motor buses and trolleybuses. I remember the trolleybuses running when we drove through Reading on our way to visit my great-aunt near Wokingham in the mid-1960s (no M4 then!), but at that young age never photographed them. I also recall the strangest-looking Bristol REs, a favourite bus of mine, that I can remember. Country services were provided, at the time of my move, by Alder Valley on former Thames Valley routes. With privatisation and the splitting up of Alder Valley into north and south, roughly corresponding to the old Thames Valley and Aldershot & District areas, Alder Valley North became The Bee Line, with a distinctive yellow livery. This was subsequently absorbed into the First Group empire. First Group's presence in Reading now is on the Railair coach service from Reading station to Heathrow Airport, a route that has seen an interesting mix of vehicles, in some ways charting the development of coaching. City of Oxford worked into Reading from Oxford jointly with Thames Valley. More recently, Go Ahead, the successor to City of Oxford, work into Reading from Didcot and Oxford under the Thames Travel brand and from High Wycombe with Carousel Buses, who took over the services when Arriva pulled out of that town. Most country services are now provided by the greatly increased Reading Buses company, with many routes, both urban and country, having their own dedicated liveries. They have also revived the Thames Valley name for some operations, as well as operating London services under the Green Line Express banner. When coach services were deregulated Reading introduced a service to Southend jointly with Southend Transport. This was later shortened to terminate at Aldgate in London. It no longer runs. Independent operation was provided mostly by the Chiltern Queens company working towards Wallingford and latterly by the greatly expanded Tillingbourne of Cranleigh. Sadly, neither operator is with us now.

Our journey through Berkshire and Hampshire starts in Reading with this view from the late 1970s. Reading Corporation 276 (NRD 276F), a Pennine-bodied Bristol RELL6G, is seen here at Reading station. Reading went over to One-Man-Operation (as it was called then) in a big way in the late 1950s, first with AEC Reliances and then in the 1960s Bristol REs with a mixture of Pennine and Strachan bodywork. Notable are the very deep windows. To someone brought up on ECW-bodied REs, these looked decidedly odd to say the least! A number of these vehicles emigrated to Malta for use at Luqa Airport.

After buying East Lancs-bodied Dennis Lolines for its double-deck requirement in the early 1960s, Reading turned to the Bristol VRTLL with Northern Counties bodywork. Sadly, I never got to photograph the Lolines in service, but here we have VRT 20 (XRD 20J) at Reading station, the main hub of local bus services.

After the Bristol VRs, Reading chose the Scania-based MCW Metropolitan, as shown here by 125 (SGM 125S), again at Station Hill, Reading, in the 1980s. Reading liked the Metropolitan sufficiently enough to buy second-hand examples from London Buses and from Tyne and Wear.

Reading was one of the few operators outside London to use the Leyland Titan TN type, buying a small number between 1979 and 1983. Vehicle 70 (SBL 70Y) is seen at Station Hill, Reading, wearing a newer, brighter livery.

When coach services were introduced by Reading Buses under the Goldline name they were worked by double-deck Leyland Titans and MCW Metrobus Mk 2s fitted with coach seats wearing a maroon and gold livery, and by vehicles such as 272 (M272 SBT), a Bova Futura, seen here on Station Hill, Reading, on 13 May 2000.

1992 saw Reading Buses, as it had now become, take over the Reading and Newbury operations of The Bee Line, one of the successors to Alder Valley. Spotted on 29 May 2001 at Reading station is MCW Metrobus 174 (HCF 174W) with Newbury Bus fleetnames.

Reading has always been a very forward-looking operator and embraced the concept of low-floor vehicles from the start. Negotiating St Mary's Butts on 22 July 2000 is Optare Solo 104 (S104 LBL), showing off its Easy Access credentials.

The takeover of services from The Bee Line led to some more unusual types, for Reading, joining the fleet. Smartly turned out in Reading livery is ECW-bodied Bristol VRT 558 (GGM 79W), at the train station in about 1993. Although Reading had operated Bristol VRs, I believe these were the only ECW-bodied vehicles to serve in the fleet.

Reading turned to Optare in a big way in the 1990s, operating most types that they produced. Seen on Broad Street on 10 January 2004 is DAF-based Optare Spectra 706 (L706 FRD). The Spectra became the standard double-decker in this period, and the fleet included second-hand examples from Eastbourne.

Reading built up a fleet of Optare Excels that numbered over sixty vehicles, including fifteen bought second-hand from Cardiff. 913 (P913 GJM) is seen on 13 May 2000 at The Forbury on the Fasttrack Park and Ride to Lodden Bridge.

The idea of routes having their own colour started around 2004, the first one to be treated being the 17 from Tilehurst to Wokingham Road, a route I recall being operated by trolleybuses. Enviro400 MMC City 715 (YP67 XCK), one of a number vehicles in the fleet powered by compressed natural gas, is seen here at St Mary's Butts on 16 April 2025.

Working on Emerald Route 6 to Whitley Wood is Enviro400 MMC 764 (YY15 OYF), seen at The Forbury on 16 April 2025.

Also at The Forbury on 16 April was Enviro300SG 410 (YR13 PNO), powered by gas and working Ruby Route 10 to Kennet Island.

Seen here in Friar Street on Little Berry route 29 to Amersham Road is Enviro200 MMC 679, (YY69 TNF), again photographed on 16 April 2025.

Reading Buses faced competition in the late 1990s when Reading Mainline started running a fleet of former London Routemasters on some routes, using route letters rather than numbers. Reading Buses took them over in 1998 and continued running the Routemasters until July 2000. Observed prior to the takeover in Broad Street is Reading Mainline 2, originally London Transport RM993, dating from 1961.

When I moved to the South East in 1974, country operations around Reading, and indeed where I lived near Guildford, were in the hands of Alder Valley, formed in 1972 by the amalgamation of Thames Valley and Aldershot & District. Their vehicles around this time could carry any one of four different liveries – Thames Valley Tilling red, Aldershot & District two-tone green, Alder Valley deep red and NBC red. Seen at the back of the rather dingy bus station in the late 1970s, ECW-bodied Bristol VR 924 (FBL 116K) is in the Alder Valley deep red but with NBC-style fleetnames.

Leaving Reading bus station sometime in the late 1970s is Alder Valley 404 (LJB 331F), an ECW-bodied Bristol RESL in full NBC livery. This bus was withdrawn from service in 1978.

Thames Valley Traction started running a coach service from Reading station to Heathrow Airport in 1967. Marketed as Railair Link, it tended to be operated by the newest coaches in the fleet. In this view, dating from about 1977/78, Alder Valley 66 (KBL 227L), an ECW-bodied Bristol RELH, is seen at the station, wearing appropriate route branding.

Alder Valley was split into north and south in the lead up to deregulation in 1986. Alder Valley North, roughly the old Thames Valley area, then became The Bee Line, adopting this yellow livery, seen on Bristol VRT 504 (XMO 541H) turning into the bus station on 22 April 1989, new to Thames Valley in 1970. This vehicle later passed to well-known operator of Bristol buses, Northern Bus, gaining the name *Constable Knapweed*.

The Bee Line's first new vehicles comprised a small batch of Northern Counties-bodied Leyland Olympians. 605 (F176 LBL) is on Station Hill, setting off to Windsor, in about 1990.

Leyland Olympian 805 (B576 LPE), seen at the back of Reading bus station on 22 April 1989, with Leyland National 323 (TBL1 67M), is one of a number Alder Valley bought for London Link services to London. I recall they were comfortable to ride on, and quite speedy.

In early 1995 a batch of Northern Counties Paladin-bodied Scania L113CRLs arrived, bringing a new, brighter livery. 818 (M818 PGM) is on Station Hill en route to Camberley in about 1997.

The Railair operation has seen various liveries over the years. In the mid-1990s The Bee Line adopted this livery, which was basically the colours of the Great Western Railway. 792 (M792 TCF), a Berkhof Excellence-bodied Scania K113CRB, one of eight delivered in 1995, is parked at Reading railway station in 1997.

New vehicles for the Fasttrack Park & Ride at this time were Scania L94UBs with Wright Axcess Floline bodies. 829 (V829 FSC) is at Reading station on 25 October 2000.

First Beeline received a batch of Volvo B12Ts with Plaxton Excalibur bodies in 1999, finished in First Group corporate livery, for the Railair service. 704 (T704 JLD) is seen laying over at Reading station on 13 May 2000.

The Railair operation is now First Berkshire's only operation in Reading. Irizar i6 25102 (YR24 OXB) is seen arriving at Reading station on 16 April 2025.

Alder Valley North's High Wycombe operations were sold to the Oxford Bus Company in 1990, services being operated as the Wycombe Bus Company. Former Alder Valley Bristol VR 1552 (HJB 459W) is seen here on Station Hill in the early 1990s.

In 1994 the Oxford Bus Company was acquired by the Go Ahead Group, who in turn sold the High Wycombe service to Arriva. Arriva The Shires 3854 (N414 NRG), a Dennis Lance with Plaxton Verde body, is seen on Station Hill on 29 May 2001.

In 2024 Arriva closed their High Wycombe depot and services were taken over by Carousel, which has been part of Go Ahead since 2012, managed by the Oxford Bus Company. Enviro400 216 (EF10 OXF) is seen here at The Forbury bound for High Wycombe on 16 April 2025.

Thames Travel was founded in 1998 and expanded quite quickly, taking over services from other companies such as Chiltern Queens. Purchased from Wright of Goring, Optare Solo X383 VVY is seen on 30 August 2001 on Station Hill.

Thames Travel was taken over by Go Ahead in 2011 as part of the Oxford Bus Company, like Carousel Buses. Arriving in Reading on service X40 from Oxford is Wright StreetDeck Ultroliner 654 (SL15 XGF), on 16 April 2025.

When thinking of independent operations in Reading the name Chiltern Queens often springs to mind. Sadly, the firm is no longer with us, having ceased operations in 2004. Laying over at Reading station in the late 1970s is OJO 835M, a Leyland Leopard with Plaxton Derwent body.

The vehicles of the Tillingbourne Bus Company appeared in Reading in the late 1990s after that company gained contracted work. Former London Country South West East Lancs-bodied Volvo B10M Citybus H683 GPF is working service 144 to Wokingham on 13 May 2000.

Tillingbourne bought F282 HOD, a Plaxton Derwent-bodied Leyland Tiger, from Thames Transit in 1996. It is seen here about two years later on Station Hill heading for Wokingham.

Seen at The Forbury, on 22 July 2000, P108 OPX is MAN 11.190 with Optare Vecta body, bound for Aldershot. Sadly, this company is no longer with us.

Bracknell

Bracknell, east of Reading, is the third largest town in Berkshire. It originated in the Middle Ages and gained in importance during the nineteenth century. In 1949 it was designated as one of a number of 'new towns'. Bus operation was in the hands of Thames Valley, which became in turn Alder Valley, Alder Valley North, The Bee Line, First Berkshire and Courtney Buses. The latter was a taxi company formed in 1973, moving into bus operation in 2000, gradually taking over a number of services from First Berkshire. They were taken over by Reading Buses, working under the name Thames Valley, in 2019.

11 miles east of Reading is Bracknell. I never got to photograph there before the advent of The Bee Line. This was originally firmly Thames Valley Traction territory. Photographed on 17 April 1989 on service to Reading, Leyland National 316 (NRD 159M) was new as Alder Valley 159.

Alder Valley North became the Berks Bucks Bus Company trading as The Bee Line. New as Alder Valley 956, Bristol VR 521 (VPF 286S) is laying over in the bus station on 17 April 1989.

In common with a lot of companies at the time of deregulation, The Bee Line built up a fleet of minibuses, the Mercedes-Benz 609D with Robin Hood body being the vehicle of choice. 168 (E464 CGM) is waiting time in the bus station on 17 April 1989.

Delivered new to Alder Valley North as 1622, 822 (D822 UTF) is a low-height ECW-bodied Leyland Olympian, one of three ordered by Southern Vectis. It's seen here laying over in Bracknell bus station on 17 April 1989.

After takeover by First Group in 1997, The Bee Line received a number of Wright-bodied Renault S75s transferred from the Centrewest operation in London. Retaining its London fleetnumber of RW49, HDZ 5449 is seen here in the newer, brighter yellow livery.

More transferees from Centrewest, this time during 1999, were a number of Dennis Darts with, I always thought, slightly retro-looking Wright Handybus bodies. 88 (JDZ 2388) is photographed on 10 April 2001 on a Bracknell local service.

First Bee Line had a small fleet of Leyland Lynxes, including two Lynx 2 models transferred from Alder Valley South in 1992. 802 (K802 CAN) is seen here in 1993.

The takeover of The Bee Line by First Group saw the arrival of vehicles in their corporate livery. In the bus station on 22 February 2000 is 825 (T825 JBL), a Scania L94UB with Wright Axcess Floline body.

Joining the fleet in 1999 were five Plaxton Premiere 320-bodied Volvo B10Ms from Kelvin Central to operate London services, marketed under the Green Line name. 746 (R346 GHS) is seen here on 22 February 2000.

First Berkshire withdrew from the Bracknell area in 2015, but carried on operating the Green Line-branded routes 702 and 703 to Windsor and London. Photographed on 18 September 2016 is 37997 (BF63 HDV), a Volvo B9TL with Wright Eclipse Gemini 2 body fitted with coach seats.

When First Berkshire withdrew from Bracknell, services passed to Reading Buses. The service to Wokingham and Bracknell was branded 'Lion' and given its own dedicated livery, in common with other Reading Buses services. Enviro400 214 (SN11 BVV) is arriving from Reading on 18 September 2016.

Services around Bracknell are now operated by Reading Buses under the Thames Valley Buses name, with the former Green Line-branded route 702 operated as 'The London Line' from Legoland to London and the 703 as 'Flightline 703' from Bracknell to London Heathrow Terminal 5. Thames Valley Services 739 (FL73 WND), an Enviro400 MMC City, is seen on 25 April 2025.

Thames Valley Buses routes around Bracknell are, like all services operated by Reading Buses, colour coded with dedicated vehicles. Working service 194 to Camberley on 25 April 2025 is Enviro200 MMC 682 (YX22 OJF).

Arriving in Bracknell on 25 April 2025 on service 53 from Wexham Park Hospital, although wearing branding for service 16, is Enviro200 659 (KX64 AEF).

Thames Valley Buses 670 (YX67 UYM) is a short Enviro200 MMC, seen here heading for Winkfield, again on 25 April 2025.

Other than the Flightline vehicles, the only Thames Valley Buses double-decker seen on this visit on 25 April 2025 was Enviro400 MMC 795 (SN66 WLK), arriving from Camberley on service 194.

Leaving the bus station on service 171, Enviro200 MMC 686 (YY73 OYN) shows the blue version of the Thames Valley livery.

Having been initially a demonstrator for Evobus, Mercedes-Benz Citaro BN09 FWR eventually arrived with White Bus Services of Winkfield. It is seen here in Bracknell bus station on 25 April 2025 laying over on service X94 from Ascot.

Emigrating to Berkshire from the far north of Scotland, SJ16 CRZ is a Volvo B8RLE with MCV Evolution body, formerly with Robertson of Shetland. Entering Bracknell bus station on 25 April 2025, it is working the X94 from Ascot.

Farnborough and Aldershot

Moving to Hampshire we come to Farnborough and Aldershot, once the domain of Aldershot & District and after that Alder Valley. This area has for many years had a large military presence, with Aldershot calling itself 'The Home of the British Army'. Farnborough, of course, is home to the biannual Farnborough Air Show, which sees a large influx of visiting coaches, as well as extra buses working the special services to the air show. On deregulation, operations in this part of the Alder Valley area were sold to Frontsource in December 1987, becoming Alder Valley South, with a green and yellow livery, later dropping South from the name. A year later the company was sold to Q-Drive, thus reuniting this area with Alder Valley North as they too were owned by Q-Drive by this point. In 1990 Q-Drive sold the Guildford and Woking area operations to Arriva and in 1992 Stagecoach took over the rest of the company as Stagecoach Hants and Surrey, with a large influx of new Mercedes-Benz minibuses, Alexander-bodied Dennis Darts and Volvo Olympians. There was never much in the way of independent operation in this area, although with deregulation Tillingbourne did build up a sizeable presence in the area before its demise.

Farnborough, in times gone by, was firmly Aldershot & District territory, followed by Alder Valley. By the time I moved to the area in the late 1980s it was Alder Valley South, although 'South' was never carried on the vehicles. They, like many operators, invested in minibuses, initially Ford Transits with Carlyle bodies. Marketed as 'Whippet', 339 (C339 RPE) is seen here at Kingsmead, the main hub of services, on 27 June 1990.

Spotted on the same day, Bristol VR 616 (GGM 86W) was delivered new to Alder Valley in 1980. It's seen here working service 22 to Aldershot from Yateley.

Alder Valley South passed to Stagecoach in 1992, who operated services under the Hants & Surrey banner. With Stagecoach came an influx of new vehicles, such as 586 (K586 ODY), a Dennis Dart with Alexander Dash body, pictured here at Kingsmead.

The Ford Transits were replaced by Mercedes-Benz 709Ds with Alexander Belfast bodies, such as 868 (K868 ODY), seen here at Kingsmead on a service to the Prospect Estate.

Transferred from Worthing at the end of 1995, 624 (L624 TDY) is a Volvo B10M-50 with Alexander PS body, fitted with dual-purpose seating, and working service 19 to Camberley.

The Bristol VRs were gradually replaced by Leyland and Volvo Olympians with Alexander RL bodies such as 315 (S315 CCD), arriving in Kingsmead on service 1 from Camberley on 22 February 2000.

The service 1 Aldershot to Camberley route was upgraded to Goldline status in 2009, receiving a fleet of Enviro300s such as 27756 (GX11 AKZ), seen here taking on passengers at Kingsmead on 5 April 2016.

With the advent of low-floor buses, the Olympians were gradually replaced by Dennis Tridents with Alexander ALX400 bodies. At Kingsmead on 5 April 2016, working service 9 from Southwood, is 18386 (MX55 KSK).

In 2016 there were still a few step-entrance vehicles hanging on, such as Alexander-bodied Volvo Olympian 16468 (S168 RET). Starting life with Stagecoach East Midland at Worksop, it is seen here at Kingsmead on 5 April.

The same day saw this Optare Solo SR, 47866 (GX13 ANR), 'Yo-yoing' between the Prospect Estate and Kingsmead.

Enviro400 MMCs took over the Stagecoach Gold service 1 in 2016. 10772 (SN66 VYT) is seen at Kingsmead on 21 February 2025.

In the later version of the Stagecoach livery, itself now being replaced, Enviro400 19099 (MX07 HLV) is at Kingsmead on service 6 to Southwood, 21 February 2025.

When Alder Valley was privatised its Guildford area operations were sold to London & Country in 1990, and its services were rebranded as Guildford & West Surrey. Returning to Woking on service 44 in the late 1990s is DSL47 (N247 VPH), a Dennis Dart SLF with East Lancs Spryte body.

After deregulation Tillingbourne Bus built up a sizeable presence in the area, operating a number of services under the 'Hobbit' name. G404 DPD is an Iveco Daily 49.10 with Carlyle body, seen on 27 June 1990.

Tillingbourne operated in the area for a number of years before its sad demise in 2001. Seen at Kingsmead on 22 February 2000 is S445 JTP, a Mercedes-Benz Vario O814D with Plaxton Beaver 2 body.

Frimley Coaches operated a service, numbered 13, from Farnborough to Fleet. Seen here at Kingsmead on 24 August 2001 is Optare MetroRider J944 JJR, formerly Go Ahead Northern 344.

Moving on to Aldershot, Alder Valley Alexander-bodied Dennis Loline III 806 (464 EOT) of 1963 is in the bus station awaiting departure to Camberley's Old Dean Estate. Originally Aldershot & District 464, this vehicle was withdrawn and scrapped in 1978. It makes an interesting comparison with the modern Alexander Dennis Enviro400 MMCs in use on the service to Old Dean in 2025.

Aldershot & District turned to AEC for their single-decker requirements from 1957 until 1968, although continuing to buy AEC coaches until 1971. Alder Valley 362 (MOR 558F), new to A & D as 558 in 1968, is a Willowbrook-bodied AEC Reliance, seen here in Aldershot bus station in around 1976. It later migrated to Scotland for further service.

Seen in the bus station in the early 1980s, Marshall-bodied AEC Reliance 381 (PHO 580G) was one of the last batch of AEC buses delivered to Aldershot & District in 1969. It was withdrawn and scrapped in 1985.

AEC Reliance 53 (VCG 600H), fitted with a handsome Duple Commander IV body, was delivered new to Aldershot & District in 1970, lasting in service until 1985. Wearing NBC 'local coach' livery, it is photographed in Halimote Road, Aldershot, outside the bus station in about 1976.

Alder Valley Bristol VR 929 (HPK 506N), of Hindhead Garage, stands next to Leyland National 246 (LPF 604P) in Aldershot bus station sometime in the late 1970s. Both vehicles are fitted with dual-purpose seating and survived in the fleet until withdrawal and scrapping in 1990 and 1993 respectively.

Alder Valley South Hestair-Duple 425 1207 (E207 EPB) is leaving the bus station on the Aldershot to London service on 24 June 1989. These vehicles were comfortable and speedy machines on which to travel as they powered up the M3 motorway.

In 1992 Alder Valley become part of Stagecoach. In 1994 former Maidstone & District Bristol VR 759 (BKE 859T) joined the fleet from Hastings & District. It is seen here laying over in Aldershot bus station. It was withdrawn in 1999.

Aldershot bus station closed in 2023 and the buses now terminate at various different points around the town, mostly some distance away from the train station. The furthest away is probably the terminus for the Stagecoach Gold service 1 to Camberley Old Dean. Enviro400 MMC 10774 (SN66 VYV) is seen here on 21 February 2025. It makes a nice contrast with the Dennis Loline pictured earlier heading to Old Dean.

Most services in Aldershot seem to terminate in Victoria Road, like service 20 to Guildford. Enviro200 36910 (GX13 APK) was photographed on 21 February 2025.

Seen at the same stop on the same day, Enviro400 19081 (MX56 FTY) is about to depart for North Town.

A chance find in Aldershot in about 1975 was this Ford R1114 with Plaxton Panorama Elite III body, PJW 789L, from the National Travel Midland fleet. Working on a National Express service here, this coach started life in the fleet of Don Everall Travel as the Wolverhampton Wanderers FC team coach.

In the late 1990s Aldershot was served by National Express on its route to Poole. Seen in Halimote Road is Bournemouth Transport 370 (N370 TJT), a Scania K113CRB with Van Hool Alizee body.

The last image of Tillingbourne Bus in this book featuring Northern Counties Paladin-bodied Dennis Dart L104 EPA leaving Aldershot bus station for Reading. The bus station had been redeveloped by this time and was a bit closer to the train station.

Winchester

Further south is the ancient city of Winchester, famous for its cathedral, which is the longest Gothic cathedral in Europe. Winchester's history goes back to pre-Roman times. Bus operation in Winchester was in the hands of the well-known King Alfred Motor Services, as well as Hants & Dorset. King Alfred was established in 1915 and by the outbreak of the Second World War had become the principal operator in Winchester with a modern up-to-date fleet. Growth continued over the years, and the company was the first to take delivery of a batch of new Metro-Scania single-deckers in 1971. In 1973 the company sold out to Hants & Dorset. With the onset of privatisation, this company was split into three smaller units: Wilts & Dorset, which I covered in a previous volume, Provincial in Gosport and Hampshire Bus in Winchester, Southampton and Basingstoke. Southampton area services were sold to Solent Blue Line, which became part of the Go Ahead Group. Nowadays bus services are in the hands of Stagecoach South and Bluestar, part of Go South Coast, with little independent operation. National Express, however, are frequent visitors to the city with services to and from London, as well as Heathrow and Gatwick airports and elsewhere in the UK. Visiting coaches are a regular sight as well.

My first visit to Winchester after moving to the South East was sadly after the days of King Alfred. However, a small number of their former vehicles were still around. Photographed in about 1979, Plaxton Derwent-bodied Leyland Panther UOU 419H had become Hants & Dorset 2699. It's seen here on The Broadway. This vehicle has since been preserved.

More normal Hants & Dorset fare, and sporting their typical sun visor over the windscreen, 1235 (KRU 235F) is of the slightly less common FLF6L variant, again seen at The Broadway.

Photographed on 19 February 1990, after the takeover by Stagecoach, but still in Hampshire Bus livery, is Bristol VR 363 (RJT 154R), leaving the bus station on a local service.

Stagecoach bought a small batch of three Dennis Javelins with Duple 300 bodies in 1989. 803 (F137 SPX), the last of the batch, is seen here on 19 February 1990, leaving the bus station for Andover.

Stagecoach Hampshire acquired three Leyland National 2s from Western National in 1989. The third member of the batch, 745 (FDV 831V), formerly WNOC 2885, is seen in St George's, Street on 19 February 1990 on a former King Alfred route.

Stagecoach Hampshire became part of Stagecoach South. In around 1990 they introduced a new livery, sometimes referred to as the 'beach ball' livery. Dennis Dart 32324 (N324 AMC), carrying an Alexander Dash body, was new to Stagecoach East London, moving to Winchester in 1998. It's seen here on a local service on 31 December 2010.

Leaving the bus station on the same day is Enviro200 36026 (GX07 HUP) on a local service to Springvale, with appropriate route branding.

Park and Ride services in Winchester have their own dedicated livery. Enviro300 27619 (GX10 HCG) is at the stop on The Broadway on 31 December 2010.

A visit to Winchester on 27 August 2011 found ADL Trident 18520 (GX06 DXU), with ADL ALX400 body, wearing 'The Rivers' branding, leaving the bus station on service 69 to Fareham.

Larger single-deckers in use were the Alexander PS-bodied Volvo B10M-50s. Here 20995 (R955 XVM) is seen leaving the bus station for Petersfield on 27 August 2011.

In 2012 there were still one or two step-entrance double-deckers around. Seen on 5 May in the city centre is Alexander RL-bodied Volvo Olympian 16282 (P282 VPN).

During 2015 Stagecoach South rebranded its Winchester city services as 'The King's City', with a fleet of new Enviro200 MMCs in a dedicated livery inspired by King Arthur. 37408 (YX65 PYA) is seen on The Broadway en route to Stanmore on 30 December 2015.

Seen the same day is Northern Counties Palatine 2-bodied Volvo Olympian 16632 (P232 VCK), one of the last step-entrance vehicles leaving the bus station on city service 3.

In 2017 new Enviro400 MMCs were introduced on service 64 to Alton. On The Broadway is 10893 (YX67 VCF) in company with King Alfred POU 494, a preserved East Lancs-bodied Leyland Titan PD2, on 1 January 2019.

During 2017 the bus station in Winchester was completely remodelled with the bus flow being reversed, the old depot building being demolished and the whole area becoming generally much lighter and more spacious. In this shot, taken on 3 August 2024, Enviro200 MMC 37417 (YX65 PYP) is entering the bus station with the Guildhall in the background. 'The King's City' livery is now a memory.

Hampshire Bus relinquished the old Hants & Dorset service 47 to Southampton via Chandlers Ford and for a period it was operated by Southampton Citybus. East Lancs-bodied Dennis Dominator 298 (F298 PTP) is seen leaving the bus station sometime in 1990.

The sale of Southampton and Eastleigh operations to Solent Blue Line brought this company into Winchester, as seen here on 19 February 1990 with ECW-bodied Bristol LHS6L 201 (LFJ 849W), formerly Western National 95, in Jewry Street.

Solent Blue Line became part of the Go Ahead Group when that organisation acquired Southern Vectis in 2005. Two years prior to this the operation had been rebranded as Bluestar. The old service 47 had been recast as service 1 with a dedicated fleet of vehicles. 1128, HF58 KCE, a Scania N230UD, is seen leaving the bus station on 27 August 2011.

The Scanias were replaced on service 1 by Enviro400s during 2013. 1529 (HJ63 JHY) is seen in Winchester bus station on 30 December 2015.

During 2016 the Enviro400s were replaced by Enviro400 MMCs, which have in turn been replaced by new 400 MMCs like 1795 (HJ25 BXW), seen here on The Broadway. The route has also been rebranded 'The One'.

First Group established a low-cost intercity coach service in 2009. The first services were between London and Southampton and Portsmouth. A fleet of refurbished Scania K114EB4 vehicles with Irizar PB bodies was used, the coaches carrying the names of women from popular American songs. 23323 (YN06 CGX), named *Sharona*, is on The Broadway on 1 January 2012. Greyhound services ceased in 2015.

National Express serve Winchester on services from London and from Heathrow Airport to the south coast. Heading for Southsea from Heathrow is Lucketts of Fareham BF68 LEJ, a Scania K410 with Caetano Levante 3 body, seen on 1 January 2019.

Mervyn's Coaches of Innersdown operated a service into Winchester from Micheldever. Seen on 30 December 2015 is 741 UKL, a more unusual Van Hool Alizee-bodied Volvo B10M-48, new to Southern of Barrhead as M40 SOU. Since this vehicle's withdrawal this registration has been transferred to a Scania coach.

Southampton

Continuing southwards we come to the port city of Southampton, a place with a rich history going back certainly to Roman times and still a thriving maritime centre with extensive docks and regular visits from cruise ships. It was the departure point for the RMS *Titanic* on its ill-fated maiden voyage, and before that the original point of departure for the Pilgrim Fathers in 1620, and the home port for such famous ships as the *Queen Elizabeth* and the *Queen Mary*. It was also where the famous Supermarine Spitfire was built. Local bus services were in the hands of Southampton Corporation Transport, becoming Southampton City Transport in 1964 with the elevation of Southampton to city status. The origins of the company go back to 1919, operating both motor buses and trams. The trams were finally abandoned in 1949. The Southampton buses that I recall were AEC Regent Vs, with particularly handsome bodies by East Lancs and its subsidiary Neepsend, and Leyland Atlanteans, also with East Lancs bodies. As a result of deregulation, an arms-length company named Southampton Citybus was formed, which was owned by the local council until 1993 when it was sold to the employees. In 1997 it was sold to First Group, who operated it as First Southampton, then as First Hampshire & Dorset. First pulled out of Southampton completely in 2023. Other services were operated by Hants & Dorset, becoming Hampshire Bus when the company was split up. It was one of the first companies to be sold after deregulation, going initially to Stagecoach in 1997. However, after a short time the Southampton operations were sold to Solent Blue Line, a company set up by Isle of Wight-based Southern Vectis. This was in turn bought by the Go Ahead Group in 2005. Services in Southampton and the surrounding area are now operated by Bluestar. The splitting up of Hants & Dorset also created Provincial, becoming People's Provincial with a company buyout in 1987. People's Provincial worked services into Southampton after deregulation and became part of First Group in 1999. It now operates around Gosport and Fareham as First Solent.

After the Bristol buses of my native West Country I've always liked AECs, particularly the Regent V. Seen here at Southampton station, appearing to almost touch the road with its rear platform, is Neepsend-bodied 393 (KOW 901F) of Southampton City Transport, photographed in 1977.

After the Regent Vs came the Leyland Atlanteans with East Lancs bodies. Laying over on Palmerston Park is 219 (ORV 89S), again photographed in 1977.

The company became an 'arms-length' company called Southampton Citybus at deregulation in 1986. In 1987 Solent Blue Line started working in competition and Citybus responded by reintroducing crew operation with former London Routemasters. For some reason I never got around to photographing them, but I did see former RM1993 (ALD 993B), 403 in the Citybus fleet, after it had entered preservation. It's at the Cobham Rally on 9 April 1989.

Southampton Council sold the company to its employees in 1993. They introduced a fleet of gas-powered Dennis Darts with Plaxton Pointer bodies, the largest such fleet in the UK. 332 (N161 GOT) is seen parked on Palmerston Park in 1996.

In 1992, Citybus purchased some Roe-bodied Leyland Atlanteans from Plymouth. 121 (STK 121T), named *Golfito*, is seen in 1996 on Vincents Walk.

Variety was added to the mostly Leyland fleet in 1993 when former Volvo B10B demonstrator K114 PRV joined the fleet. Numbered 114, it had a Northern Counties Paladin body and is seen here at Palmerston Park in 1996.

In 1997 First Group acquired Citybus, becoming First Southampton, and later part of First Hampshire & Dorset. Seen in the low winter sunshine on 27 January 2001, East Lancs-bodied Leyland Atlantean YRV 254V has become 1254, and still wears its red Citybus livery.

Articulated buses, in the form of Wright Fusion-bodied Volvo B7LAs, appeared in Southampton in 2000/1. Seen at Palmerston Park on 7 February 2004 is 147 (Y147 ROT).

More usual Volvo single-deckers were the Wright Renown-bodied B10BLEs delivered in 1998. 1121 (S121 JTP) is seen at Palmerston Park on 27 January 2001.

Double-deckers included Alexander ALX400-bodied Dennis Tridents like 808 (W808 EOW), seen at Palmerston Park on 27 January 2001. First Group invested in new buses for Southampton during 2014, but unfortunately I never got to photograph them. They withdrew completely from Southampton in 2022.

The only Hants & Dorset vehicle I ever photographed in Southampton was Bristol VR 3373 (RPR 719R), seen at the train station in 1977.

In 1987, Solent Blue Line bought the Southampton and Eastleigh operations of Hampshire Bus from Stagecoach. That year also saw the company start to compete with Citybus on some city services. Seen in Bargate Street on 24 June 1992, former Hants & Dorset Bristol VR 87 (RPR 717R) is seen on city service 19 to Thornhill.

Minibuses featured in the Solent Blue Line fleet, such as Iveco Daily 49.10s with uncommon bodywork by Car Chairs. 233 (J233 KDL) is seen at Hanover Buildings on 24 June 1992.

Seen at West Quay on 7 February 2004, 757 (HX51 ZRK) is a Volvo B7TL with East Lancs Vyking body.

Laying over on Castle Way on 7 February 2004 was DAF SB120 with Wright Cadet body 551 (YG52 CME). In the earlier days of low-floor buses operators were keen to advertise the fact on their vehicles.

In 2005 Solent Blue Line was bought by the Go Ahead Group under the Go South Coast banner. From 2008 services were run under the name Bluestar. Seen at West Quay on 28 August 2011 is East Lancs Vyking-bodied Volvo B7TL 782 (HX51 ZRD), from the same batch as 757 seen earlier.

Single-deckers joining the fleet included Mercedes-Benz Citaros like 444 (HX06 EZD), seen at West Quay on 28 August 2011 bound for Hythe.

Later single-deckers comprised Enviro200 MMCs like 220 (HF67 EUA), letting passengers off in Above Bar Street on 14 March 2025.

6941 (LX58 CYA), an ADL Trident 2 with Optare Olympus body, started life with London General. It's photographed passing Hanover Buildings on 14 March 2025.

Like so many major towns and cities now, Southampton does not have a bus station any more. At the Hanover Buildings terminus of service 1 from Winchester on 14 March 2025 is Enviro400 MMC 1797 (HJ25 BXY).

Working into Southampton from Gosport, People's Provincial was the third portion of Hants & Dorset. Passing the Bargate in 1995 was Bristol VR 516 (RHT 503S), bought from Bristol Omnibus in 1994.

Wilts & Dorset worked into Southampton from Salisbury. This company became part of Go South Coast in 2003. On 7 February 2004, Plaxton Premiere 320-bodied DAF SB3000 3214 (R214 NFX) was loading on Castle Way for its return run.

West Quay is the location again for More Enviro400 1535 (HJ63 JJO), on service 6 to Lymington on 14 March 2025. The More name is used by Go South Coast for services in the Bournemouth and Poole area.

Gosport

Travelling eastwards from Southampton and then south from Fareham along the permanently congested A32 we come to Gosport, once the domain of the Gosport and Fareham Omnibus Company, trading as Provincial. It is, I think, fair to say this firm had a somewhat individual approach to its choice of vehicles, rebodying frequently and trying out air-cooled engines. Acquisition by the National Bus Company in 1970 led to more common types of vehicles entering the fleet, such as Bristol REs and the inevitable Leyland Nationals. I never got to photograph this fleet until after deregulation when it had become People's Provincial. The First Solent depot at Hoeford is home now to a sizeable fleet of electric buses. A new bus station has opened in recent months at Gosport Ferry, the long-time terminus of Provincial services.

Seen in Gosport bus station is Leyland National 31 (JBP 131P) of People's Provincial, in their initial privatisation livery.

People's Provincial adopted a smart green and cream livery, as shown here on Bristol VR 509 (SFJ 101R), purchased from Western National in 1993, leaving Gosport bus station. Leyland National 22 (PCG 922M) is in the initial privatisation livery.

New vehicles also joined the fleet, such as 604 (N604 EBP,) a Dennis Dart with less-common UVG UrbanStar bodywork.

Provincial became part of First Group in 1995 and adopted a red and cream livery, examples of which will be seen later in this book. In 2012 First Hampshire & Dorset started the 'Eclipse' service between Fareham and Gosport, part of which ran along a dedicated busway that followed the trackbed of the old railway line to Gosport. The first vehicles used on this route were Volvo B7RLEs with Wright Eclipse Urban 2 bodies, such as 69551 (BF12 KWN), seen here leaving Gosport bus station on 23 July 2012.

The Volvos were replaced in 2016 by Enviro200 MMCs like 67184 (YX66 WCA), here heading for Fareham on 31 December 2019.

The main bus terminal in Gosport was Gosport Ferry, near where the ferries cross the Solent to Portsmouth depart. In 1972 a new bus station was built, the one seen in the previous pictures. In 2024 another new bus station was opened, which is seen here with Wrightbus GB Kite Electroliner BEV 63697 (LV74 EYR), reversing off-stand on an Eclipse working to Fareham on 13 March 2025. The Electroliners entered service during 2024, replacing the Enviro200 MMCs.

Another Electroliner seen on 13 March 2025, this time in First Solent livery, was 63601 (BK73 AMX), here working service 9 to Fareham.

There isn't much double-deck operation in Gosport. However, they do occasionally appear, like Wright StreetDeck 35164 (SK65 PWJ) heading for Alverstoke on service 11.

The only vehicles in First Group livery observed on my visit on 13 March 2025 were Wright StreetLites like 47592 (SN14 ECW), entering the bus station on service 5.

Portsmouth and Southsea

Continuing eastwards along the A27 we come to the city of Portsmouth and its neighbour Southsea, our final stop. Portsmouth has a long history as an important naval base and is home to Nelson's flagship HMS *Victory*. More modern ships of the Royal Navy can frequently be seen here. The Hard is the main bus station for Portsmouth with connections for national rail services and ferries to Gosport and the Isle of Wight. Urban services in Portsmouth and Southsea were provided exclusively by Portsmouth Corporation Transport until 1988. This firm commenced motor bus operation in 1919. Trams were operated until the 1930s and trolleybuses between 1934 and 1963. Leylands were the vehicles of choice with Titans, Atlanteans, Leopards, Panther Cubs and Nationals being operated. Some variation was provided by AEC Swifts in the late 1960s. Portsmouth Corporation became Portsmouth City Transport in 1987. That year a new company, Red Admiral, owned jointly by Southampton Citybus and Badgerline, appeared in competition. Portsmouth City Transport was privatised in 1988 and was sold to a consortium of employees and Southampton Citybus, becoming Portsmouth Citybus. Red Admiral became a subsidiary company. Out-of-town services were provided by Southdown Motor Services, after 1970 part of the National Bus Company. Both firms were acquired by Stagecoach in 1989, who were then made to divest itself of most of the Portsmouth operation in 1989, selling it to Transit Holdings, who traded as Blue Admiral and also revived the Red Admiral name, in 1991, using a fleet of minibuses. People's Provincial also expanded into Portsmouth at this time. Transit Holdings and People's Provincial were both acquired by First Group in the mid-1990s and now operate most of the city services and routes to Fareham and Gosport. Other services are operated by Stagecoach South.

The final stop on this excursion to Berkshire and Hampshire is the maritime city of Portsmouth and nearby Southsea. I visited in 1977 on the occasion of the Silver Jubilee review of the fleet, when every available bus was pressed into service. Parked on the front at Southsea, near South Parade Pier, Portsmouth Corporation 203 (203 BTP), a 1963 Leyland Atlantean with Metro-Cammell body, was nearing the end of its time in the fleet, being withdrawn in October 1978.

Portsmouth moved away from Leyland in 1969 with a batch of Marshall-bodied AEC Swifts. 186 (NTP 186H) is seen here on the seafront at Southsea.

Unusual additions to the Portsmouth fleet in 1971 were Leyland Atlanteans with single-deck Seddon bodywork. 192 (TBK 192K) is parked on Southsea front in 1977.

Portsmouth turned to Alexander for their subsequent deliveries of Atlanteans. Again caught on the seafront at Southsea, 263 (VTP 263L) is seen heading for Paulsgrove on service 3.

Seen at The Hard Interchange, the main hub of services with bus/train/ferry connections in Portsmouth, on 27 May 1989 and carrying Portsmouth Citybus fleetnames is another uncommon vehicle in the shape of Wadham Stringer Vanguard-bodied Dennis Lancet 95 (GTP 95X).

Seen the same day at The Hard is Red Admiral E945 LAE, a Robin Hood-bodied Iveco Daily 49.10 transferred from Badgerline.

People's Provincial expanded into Portsmouth and Southsea. Open-top Bristol VR 594 (MOD 571P) is seen here on Southsea seafront in the early 1990s. This vehicle, new to Western National, travelled extensively and is now preserved at the Swansea Bus Museum.

Additional open-toppers were sourced from Bournemouth Yellow Buses in the form of two 1976 Leyland Fleetlines with Alexander bodies. 591 (NFX 130P) is on Southsea seafront on 28 July 1992.

People's Provincial 402 (THX 248S) is a short 10.3-metre Leyland National bought in 1991 from London Buses and seen here in Southsea on 28 July 1992.

Minibuses also figured in People's Provincial operations. Marshall-bodied Iveco Daily 49.10 143 (J143 KPX) is in Southsea, leading a similar vehicle.

When Transit Holdings took over the Portsmouth Citybus operations they revived the Red Admiral name for services that ran outside the city boundary. Carlyle-bodied Mercedes-Benz 811D 387 (H178 GTA) is seen in Southsea on 28 July 1992.

Transit Holdings used the Blue Admiral name for services within the city boundary. Mellor-bodied Iveco Daily 49.10 2035 (L324 BOD), unusually for a minibus with dual-door body, is in Southsea bound for Paulsgrove in about 1994.

Although being a minibus operation, Blue Admiral did retain former Portsmouth Metro-Cammell-bodied Leyland Titan PD2 LRV 992, dating from 1956 and seen here on the seafront at Southsea in 1991.

When First Group took over both People's Provincial and the former Portsmouth Citybus operation in 1996, they adopted a red and cream livery. Leyland National 2 409 (WAS 766V) was transferred to First Provincial from Kelvin Central in Scotland in 1996. It's seen here at The Hard, Portsmouth, on 10 August 2000, with the masts of HMS *Victory* in the background.

First Provincial retained open-top buses, converting this dual-door Bristol VR, 504 (RHT 504S), formerly Bristol Omnibus 5110. On 10 August 2000 it was working service 50 to Eastney.

By 2011 First Group corporate livery reigned and operations were under the First Hampshire & Dorset banner. Seen at The Hard on 10 September is Scania CN94UB 65019 (YN54 NZT).

Again at The Hard on 10 September 2011, First Hampshire & Dorset 69395 (HY09 AZF) is a Volvo B7RLE with Wright Eclipse Urban 2 body. It's carrying route branding for service 41 to Clanfield.

Operating on the Tipner Park & Ride on 7 June 2015 was this First Hampshire & Dorset Dennis Trident with East Lancs Lolyne body, 32764 (WJ55 CSO), and carrying Solent fleetnames. My partner and I were using the Park & Ride that day to visit the Southdown Centenary Rally in Southsea.

First moved away from the 100 per cent corporate image during the 2010s and rolled out brands such as 'The Star', as featured on Wright StreetLite Max DF 63049 (SK63 KJA), seen on 11 June 2017 at The Hard, Portsmouth.

Seen opposite the interchange on 11 June 2017, First Hampshire & Dorset Wright StreetLite DF 63306 (SN65 OLK) carries a livery and route branding for Solent Ranger service X4 to Southampton.

The Park & Ride service is now in the hands of a number of Wright StreetDecks transferred from First Leeds. First Hampshire & Dorset 35619 (YJ70 BGZ) is seen on 14 May 2025 in the transport interchange that was extensively remodelled in 2017.

Working 'The Star' service 7 is route-dedicated Enviro200 MMC YX69 NSN, numbered 67275 in the First Hampshire & Dorset fleet and seen on 14 May 2025 at the interchange.

Portsmouth did have an extensive trolleybus system, which ceased in 1963, long before I first picked up a camera! However, electric buses are again serving the streets of Portsmouth and Southsea in the shape of First Hampshire & Dorset Wrightbus GB Kite Electroliner BEVs, exemplified here by 63610 (BK73 AOC), seen on 14 May 2025 at South Parade Pier, Southsea.

Most of the First Hampshire & Dorset Wrightbus Electroliners that work into Portsmouth and Southsea carry the blue 'First Solent' livery. However, those branded for the 'Eclipse' Fareham to Gosport service occasionally stray from their usual haunt, as seen here with 63690 (LV24 EYH) at The Hard Interchange in Portsmouth on 14 May 2025 on service 3 to South Parade Pier.

A major provider of services in the Portsmouth area was Southdown Motor Services, a name that will always conjure up images of their fleet of handsome full-fronted Northern Counties-bodied Leyland Titan PD3s. 402 (402 DCD), a convertible open-top variant, is seen here in Southsea on a special service in connection with the Queen's Silver Jubilee review of the fleet in 1977.

Also working a special service for the fleet review is PD3 250 (GUF 250D). As far as I know this was the only PD3 in the fleet to have the curved BET-style windscreen, although the 1967 delivery did have this windscreen on the upper-deck together with the panoramic windows.

Still connected with the fleet review, Northern Counties-bodied Leyland Leopard 452 (NUF 452G) is parked here in Southsea. I believe this style of body was unique to Southdown.

With privatisation, Southdown was sold as a management buyout in 1987, using a livery similar to the original, very smart Southdown livery. Bristol VR 274 (JWV 274W) is seen here on 27 May 1989 at The Hard Interchange having just arrived on the long 700 Coastliner service from Brighton.

Stagecoach transferred vehicles to the south coast from elsewhere in its empire, such as 656 (416 DCD), a Volvo B10M-55 with Alexander PS body, arriving from Ribble in Lancashire. Originally registered L346 KCK, it received the registration of one of Southdown's PD3s in 1995. It was photographed in 1995 in Southsea.

Stagecoach Hampshire Bus reached Portsmouth and Southsea with the 69 service from Winchester. Alexander-bodied Leyland Olympian 206 (F606 MSL) is seen here in Southsea. Nowadays the 69 service runs from Winchester to Fareham.

Seen in late 1994 on the Coastliner 700 is 245 (L245 SDY), a Volvo Olympian with Northern Counties Palatine 1 body, arriving at The Hard Interchange.

Stagecoach transferred a number of former London Leyland Titan TN15s to the former Southdown operation. 7214 (OHV 784Y) is at The Hard on 10 August 2000 heading for Havant.

The same day Volvo B10M-55 648 (R648 HCD), fitted with a Northern Counties Paladin body, is heading for Southsea from Winchester.

In 1999 Stagecoach bought a batch of three-year-old Dennis Darts with Plaxton Pointer bodies from Hong Kong Citybus. A number found their way to Sussex Coastline, as the former Southdown operation was now called. Registered N977 RCD, 430 gained the registration 400 DCD from one of the Titan PD3s. It was caught at The Hard, Portsmouth, on 10 August 2000.

Arriving on the same day from Brighton on the Coastliner 700 service, Volvo Olympian 324 (S324 CCD) has Alexander RL bodywork and is working right through to Southsea.

In Stagecoach's second corporate livery is Stagecoach South Enviro300 27565 (GX58 GNO). It carries route branding for local service 23 to Leigh Park and is seen here on 11 June 2017 entering the remodelled interchange.

Arriving at The Hard Interchange on 11 June 2017 with its destination set for return to Chichester on the Coastliner 700 is Stagecoach South Enviro400 19063 (MX56 FSP).

In 1965 a hovercraft service was introduced between Southsea and Ryde on the Isle of Wight. That service still operates today and claims to be the world's oldest all-year hovercraft service. A bus service from the terminal at Southsea to The Hard Interchange was introduced and in the 2010s was being operated by Stagecoach South, who took over the service from Tellings-Golden Miller in about 2009. One vehicle is allocated to the service and in 2011 the dedicated vehicle was 33156 (LK55 KZZ), a Dennis Dart SLF with Plaxton Pointer 2 body that came from Tellings.

In 2024, First Hampshire and Dorset took over the operation of Hoverbus and allocated Enviro200 MMC 67198 (YX67 UZC) to the service. It is seen here on 14 May 2025 arriving at The Hard Interchange.

A visit to Portsmouth in the late 1990s found Western National 2258 (H613 UWR) taking on passengers at The Hard on its way to Helston on National Express 315 from Brighton. A Volvo B10M-60 with Plaxton Paramount 3500 Mk III body, it was acquired by Western National from Wallace Arnold in 1994.

National Express routes around Portsmouth nowadays consist of services to London. Luckett's of Fareham operate a number of routes for National Express, as seen here by FN62 CWD, a Volvo B9R with Caetano Levante body arriving at The Hard on 11 June 2017 on its way to London.

Departing The Hard Interchange for Chichester, the starting point for the next book in the series, on the Coastliner 700 on 14 May 2025 is Stagecoach South Enviro400 MMC 11588 (YX23 OPP). The remodelled interchange can be seen in this view, together with the masts of HMS *Warrior*, Britain's first iron-clad warship.